Traditional Arabesque

TEXTILE DESIGN II

PAGE ONE PUBLISHING

Original title "Textile Design in Japan: Traditional Arabesque"
© 1977 by Kamon Yoshimoto
First published in Japan by Graphic-sha Publishing Co., Ltd., Tokyo, Japan

© 1993 for this edition: Page One Publishing Pte Ltd., Singapore

Distributed worldwide (except Japan) by
Könemann Verlagsgesellschaft mbH, Bonner Str.126, D-50968 Köln
Edited by Kamon Yoshimoto
Owned by Research Association for Old Textiles

Printed in Singapore
ISBN 981 - 00 - 4774 - 6

Contents

KARAKUSA - MONYO patterns

Inhaltsverzeichnis

KARAKUSA - MONYO - Muster

Table des matières

Motifs KARAKUSA - MONYO

Traditional japanese arabesque patterns

Kamon Yoshimoto

KARAKUSA (arabesque) patterns, in general, are made up of circular and elliptical shapes of stems and leaves drawn by an unlimited number of diagonal lines of simple and defined patterns, thus creating an image of endlessly linked forms.

This simple type of KARAKUSA pattern can still be seen today on fabrics for items such as FUROSHIKI, ticks, and various types of bags which have become an integral part of people's daily life, so that it has become one of the most commonly used patterns in Japan.

The popularity of the KARAKUSA patterns which we see today dates from the second half of the Edo period (1604-1867). The patterns were first introduced into this country during the Asuka (592-710) and the Nara (711-794) periods, through trade with the Chinese mainland. The original pattern was called KARAKUSA, followed by the more decorative patterns of "RENGE" and "UNGYO" which were mostly worn by court nobles, aristocrats and priests.

With the advent of the Kamakura period (1192-1333) and with the samurai classes gaining more and more power, the samurai began to use these patterned fabrics for both their everyday clothing as well as for their armour. When the tea ceremony began to flourish, the import of luxurious materials and SARASA cloth dyed with KARAKUSA and SOKA patterns was greatly supported by feudal lords, samurai and persons of sophisticated taste. Even some of the rich merchants who were on good terms with feudal lords and samurai wore luxurious apparel which eventually spread to the common people as a new fashion.

As peace reigned over the land, the shogunate, during the second half of the Edo period, issued proclamations to the public from time to time warning them against indulging in luxury. As a consequence, the public began wearing cotton instead of silk garments. The big question then was how cotton fabric could be made to look beautiful and how it could be worn with refinement. The indigo KARAKUSA was taken up as a new fashion for KARAKUSA patterns which gained popularity in Edo (Tokyo), Kyoto, and finally made its way throughout the country. The KARAKUSA pattern was adopted for fabrics used for making articles such as mattresses, ticks, clothing, FUROSHIKI, etc., and became a part of people's daily life.

This literature was compiled and printed with the purpose and in the hope of preserving the history of KARAKUSA patterns which flourished in the days of our predecessors and were especially popular among the general public. Since the end of World War II, the use of traditional patterns has begun to decline rapidly. Therefore, in order to preserve the patterns, it is our intention to publish a reproduced version of the KARAKUSA patterns with a modern touch so that the reader might acquire a better understanding of their uniqueness in the hope that they might influence modern decorative design.

This book contains the following five categories, with a total of over 550 patterns.

1. Indigo arabesque patterns (stencil-dyed) 108 patterns
2. Arabesque patterns on brocade, satin, in gobelin technique, etc. 154 patterns
3. SARASA arabesque patterns 156 patterns
4. Arabesque patterns (YUZEN type, dyed) 66 patterns
5. Clothing for home use and everyday wear (YUKATA type, stencil-dyed) 68 patterns

Traditionelle japanische Arabeskenmuster

Kamon Yoshimoto

KARAKUSA - Muster (Arabesken) bestehen im allgemeinen aus Stengeln und Blättern in runder und elliptischer Form, die zahllose diagonale Streifen mit einem einfachen und genau definierten Muster bilden, so daß das Bild eines endlos zusammenhängenden Musters entsteht.

Dieses einfache KARAKUSA-Muster findet sich heute noch auf Stoffen für FUROSHIKI (Einschlagtücher), Bezüge und verschiedene Arten von Taschen und ist so zu einem festen Bestandteil des täglichen Lebens geworden. Ohne übertreiben zu wollen, kann man sagen, daß es sich bei diesem Muster um eines der gebräuchlichsten in Japan handelt. Der Grundstein für die allgemeine Beliebtheit des KARAKUSA - Musters wurde in der Mitte der Edozeit (1604-1867) gelegt. Es wurde in der Asukazeit (592-710) und in der Narazeit (711-794) durch den Handel mit dem chinesischen Festland in Japan eingeführt. Das Originalmuster wurde KARAKUSA genannt. Es gab aber auch die schmuckvolleren Ausführungen „RENGE" und „UNGYO", die zu jener Zeit vor allem von Höflingen, Aristokraten und Priestern getragen wurden.

Mit Beginn der Kamakurazeit (1192-1333) und dem Aufstieg der an die Macht gelangenden Samuraiklassen wurden diese Muster von den Samurai sowohl für ihre Alltagskleidung als auch für ihre Rüstungen benutzt. Als die Teezeremonie immer beliebter wurde, förderten Feudalherren, Samurai und Menschen mit erlesenem Geschmack den Import luxuriöser Materialien und mit KARAKUSA- und SOKA-Mustern gefärbte SARASA - Stoffe. Selbst einige der reichen Kaufleute, die gute Beziehungen zu den Feudalherren und Samurai pflegten, trugen diese luxuriöse Kleidung, die schließlich von der breiten Öffentlichkeit als neue Mode übernommen wurde.

Als Frieden im Land herrschte, ergingen vom Schogunat in der Mitte der Edozeit von Zeit zu Zeit Ermahnungen an das Volk, sich nicht dem Luxus hinzugeben. Daraufhin begann das Volk, Kleidung aus Baumwolle anstatt aus Seide zu tragen. Dabei stellte sich vor allem die Frage, wie Baumwollstoffen ein prachtvolles Aussehen verliehen und wie sie geschmackvoll getragen werden könnten. Indigogefärbte Stoffe mit KARAKUSA - Muster kamen als neue Mode auf und wurden in Edo (Tokio), Kyoto und schließlich im ganzen Land beliebt. Das KARAKUSA - Muster fand sich auf Matrazen, Bezügen, Kleidungsstücken, Einschlagtüchern usw. wieder und wurde fester Bestandteil im Leben des japanischen Volkes.

Diese Informationen wurden zusammengestellt und gedruckt, um die Geschichte des KARAKUSA - Musters zu bewahren, das bei unseren Vorfahren eine Blütezeit erlebte und vor allem beim Volk weit verbreitet war. Nach dem Ende des Zweiten Weltkriegs gerieten traditionelle Muster schnell in Vergessenheit. Um die Muster zu bewahren, war es daher unsere Absicht, eine Reproduktion der KARAKUSA - Muster in modernem Stil zu veröffentlichen, so daß der Leser ihre Einzigartigkeit besser zu schätzen lernt. Außerdem hoffen wir, daß sie einigen Einfluß auf modernes Design ausüben mögen.

Dieses Buch umfaßt die fünf folgenden Kategorien mit insgesamt über 550 verschiedenen Mustern

1. Arabesken in Indigo (Schablonendruck) 108 Muster
2. Arabesken auf Brokat, Satin, als Gobelin, usw. 154 Muster
3. SARASA - Arabesken 156 Muster
4. Arabesken (YUZEN - Typ, gefärbt) 66 Muster
5. Haus- und übliche Alltagskleidung (YUKATA - Typ, mit Schablone hergestellt) 68 Muster

Motifs traditionnels japonais d'arabesques

Kamon Yoshimoto

Les motifs d'arabesques KARAKUSA sont généralement constitués de tiges de fleurs et de feuilles circulaires et elliptiques. Celles-ci forment des lignes diagonales grâce à des motifs simples et définis, donnant l'impression d'un motif infini. Ce simple motif KARAKUSA est, de nos jours, imprimé sur des tissus tels que le FUROSHIKI, le coutil, différents genres de sacs et est devenu partie intégrante de la vie quotidienne. Sans exagérer, on peut dire que c'est l'un des motifs le plus couramment utilisé au Japon.

La popularité actuelle des motifs KARAKU-SA a commencé au milieu de l'ère Edo (1604-1867). Il a été introduit dans ce pays durant les ères Asuka (592-710) et Nara (711-794) par des échanges commerciaux avec le continent chinois. Le motif original s'appelait KARAKUSA, suivi des motifs plus décoratifs «RENGE» et «UNGYO», qui étaient portés principalement par les nobles de la cour, les aristocrates et les prêtres.

Au début de l'ère Kamakura (1192-1333), les Samouraï arrivés au pouvoir commencèrent à utiliser ces motifs aussi bien pour leurs vêtements ordinaires que pour leur armure.

Lorsque la cérémonie du thé devint plus populaire, les seigneurs féodaux, les Samouraï et les personnes de bon goût favorisèrent l'importation de tissus luxueux et des tissus SARASA teints avec les motifs KARAKUSA et SOKA. Même certains des marchands riches, en bons termes avec les seigneurs féodaux et les Samouraï, portaient ces vêtements luxueux qui, finalement furent adoptés par le peuple comme une nouvelle mode.

Lorsque la paix régnait sur le pays, au milieu de l'ère Edo, le shogunate s'adressait au peuple de temps en temps, l'admonestant de ne pas s'adonner au luxe. C'est la raison pour laquelle le peuple a commencé à porter des vêtements de coton au lieu de vêtement de soie. La grande question était alors de savoir comment les tissus en coton pourraient être fabriqués de manière à paraître magnifiques et à être portés avec raffinement. Le KARAKUSA indigo a été accueilli comme une nouvelle mode et gagna sa popularité à Edo (Tokyo), Kyoto et finalement, dans tout le pays. Le motif KARAKUSA fut adopté pour des tissus tels que le coutil, les vêtements, le furoshiki, etc… et a commencé à faire partie de la vie des japonais.

Cette documentation a été compilée et publiée dans le but et l'espoir de préserver l'histoire des motifs KARAKUSA ayant connu une apogée et ayant été très répandus chez nos ancêtres. Après la fin de la 2nde guerre mondiale, les motifs traditionnels ont été rapidement oubliés. Notre intention était, avec la publication du motif KARAKUSA dans un style plus moderne, de préserver celui-ci et de faire apprécier à nos lecteurs son unicité. Nous espérons aussi qu'il aura quelque influence sur le design moderne.

Ce livre comprend les cinq catégories suivantes, avec au total plus de 550 motifs différents.

1. Arabesques en indigo (teint au patron) 108 motifs
2. Arabesques sur brocart, satin, gobelin, etc. 154 motifs
3. Arabesques SARASA 156 motifs
4. Arabesques (de type YUZEN, de couleur) 66 motifs
5. Vêtements d'intérieur et ordinaires (de type YUKATA, teint au patron) 68 motifs

**Examples of KARAKUSA - MONYO - Cho patterns
(KARAKUSA pattern book)**

**Beispiele für KARAKUSA - MONYO - Cho - Muster
(KARAKUSA - Musterheft)**

**Exemples de motif KARAKUSA - MONYO - Cho
(cahier d'échantillons KARAKUSA)**

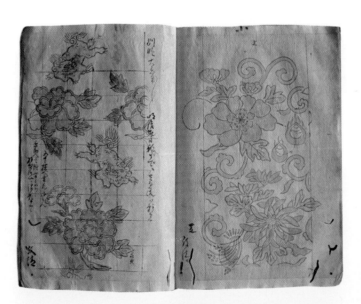

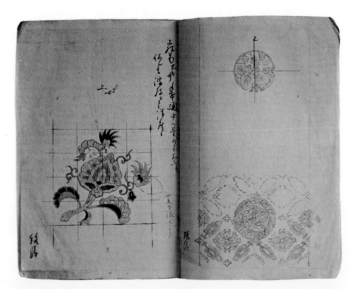

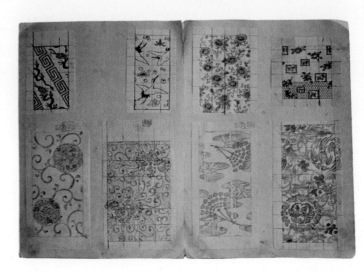

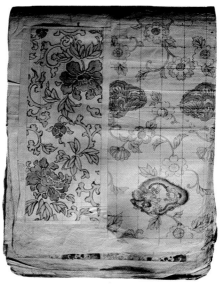

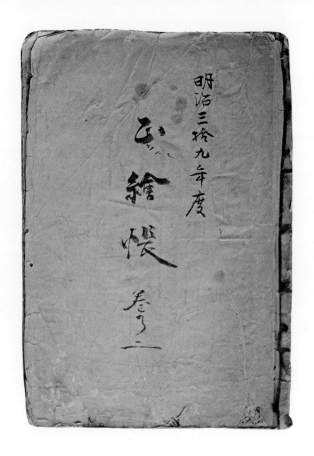

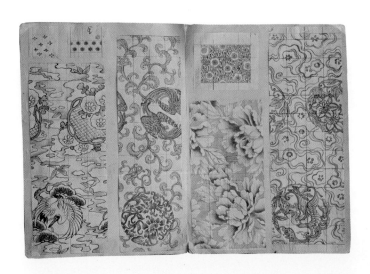

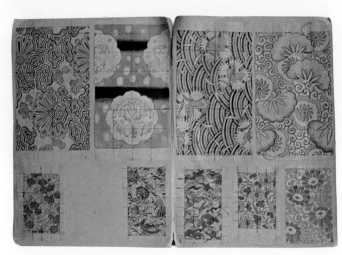

Example of original cloth with medium-sized motifs used
for everyday clothing of the common people

Originalbeispiel für Stoffe mit mittelgroßen Mustern für die
Alltagskleidung der bürgerlichen Schicht

Exemple de tissus d'origine avec des motifs de
taille moyenne pour les vêtements ordinaires
de la classe bourgeoise

Indigo arabesque patterns
(stencil-dyed)

Arabesken in Indigo
(Schablonendruck)

Arabesques en indigo
(teint au patron)

1

2

4

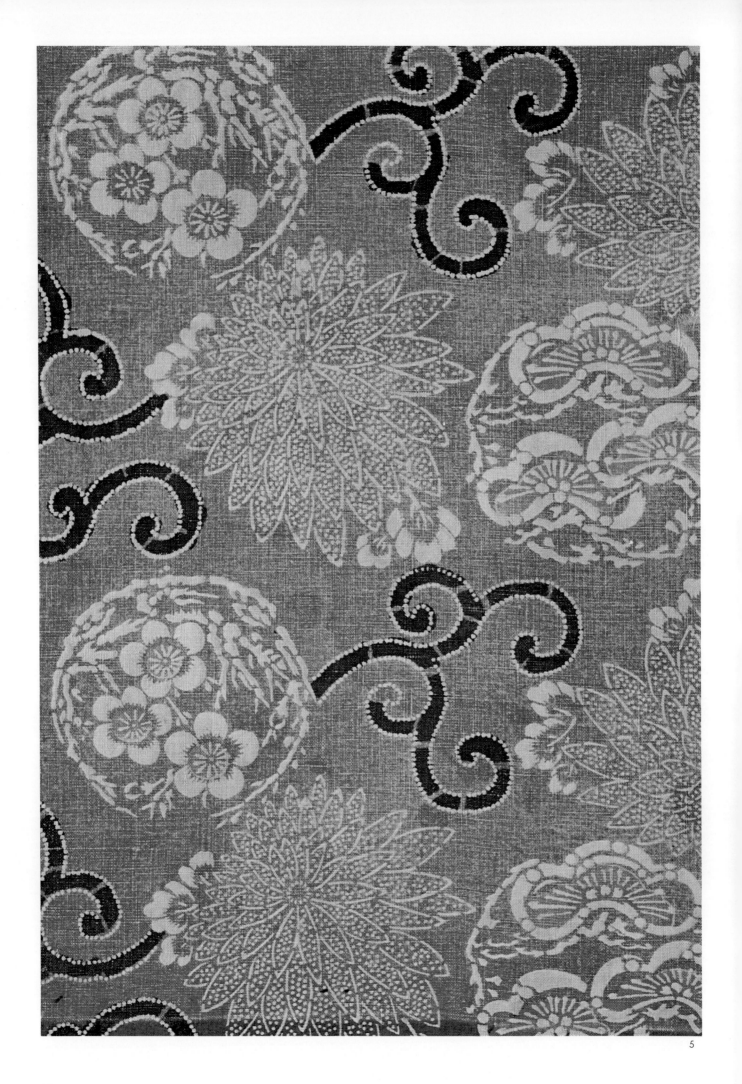

6

11

12

13

14

15

16

17

18

19

20

23

24

25

26

27

28

29

30

31

32

33

34

34

35

36

37

38

36

39

40

41

42

43

44

45

46

47

48

49

50

42

51

52

53

54

55

56

57

58

59

60

61

62

63

64

65

66

67

68

69

70

71

72

73

74

75

76

77

78

79

80

81

82

83

84

85

86

87

88

89

90

91

92

93

94

95

96

97

98

99

100

101

102

103

104

105

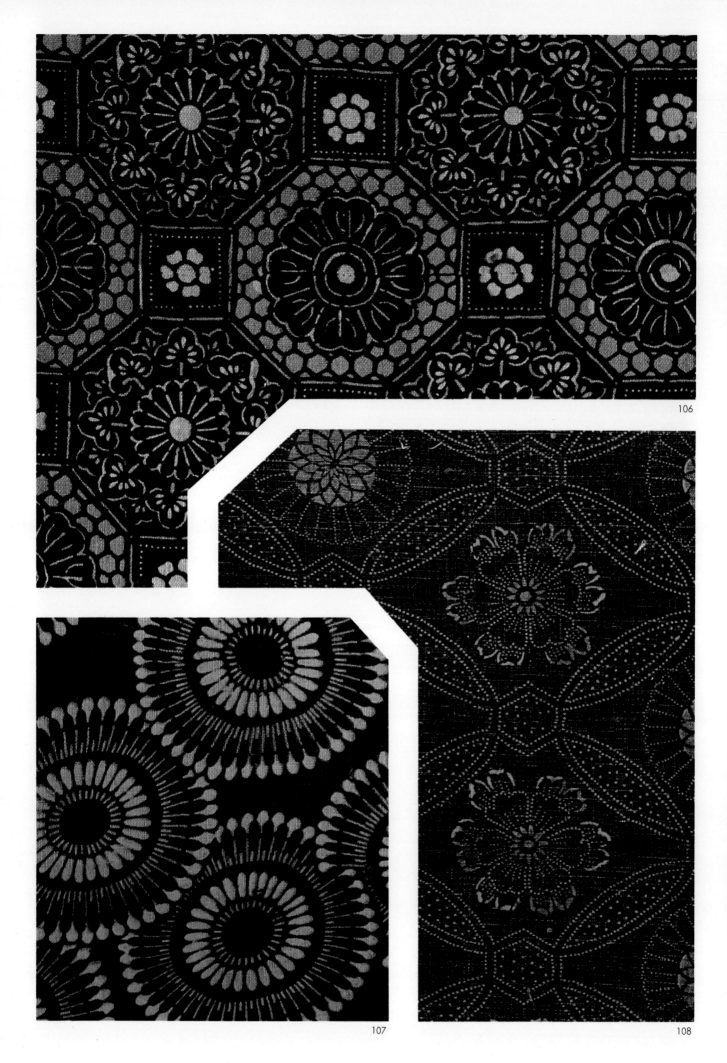

106

107

108

Arabesques
sur brocart, satin, gobelin

109

110

111

112

113

114

115

116

117

118

119

120

121

122

123

124

125

126

127

128

129

130

131

132

133

134

135

136   137   138   139   140

141

142

143

144

145

146

147

148

149

150

151

152

153

154

155

156

157

158

159

160

161

162

163

164

165

166

168

167

169

170

171

172

173

174

175

176

177

178

179

180

181

182

183

184

185

186

187

188

189

190

191

192

193

194

195

196

197

198

199

200

212

213

214

215

216

217

218

219

220

221

222

223

224

225

226

227

228

229

230

231

232

233 234 235

236 237 238 239 240 241

242

243

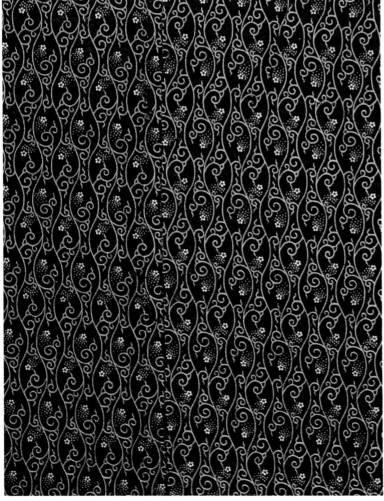

244

245

250

251

252

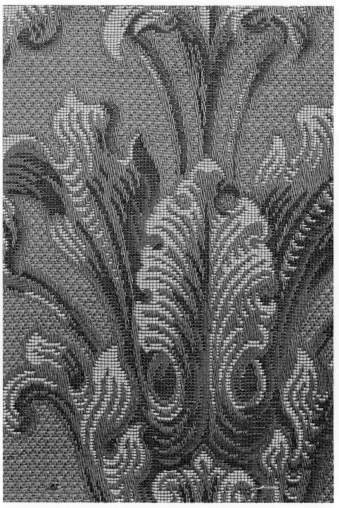

253

254

255

256

257

258

259

260

261

262

SARASA arabesque patterns

SARASA - Arabesken

Arabesques SARASA

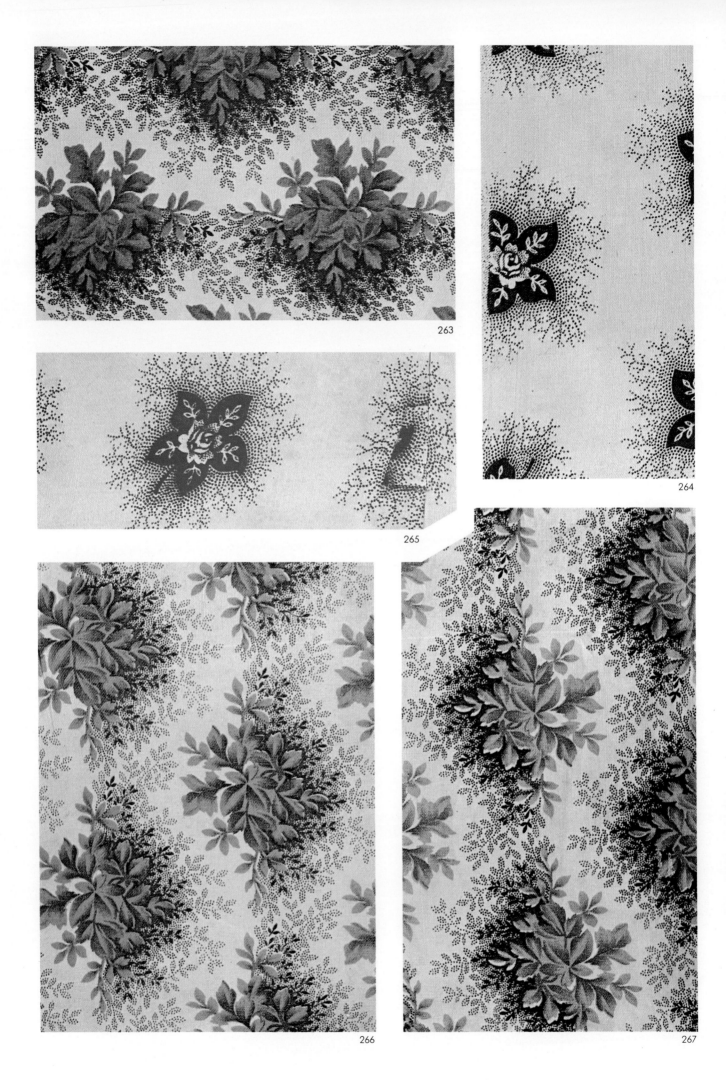

263

264

265

266

267

268

269

270

271

272

273

274

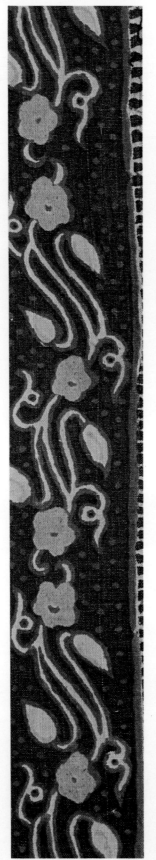

275

276

277

278

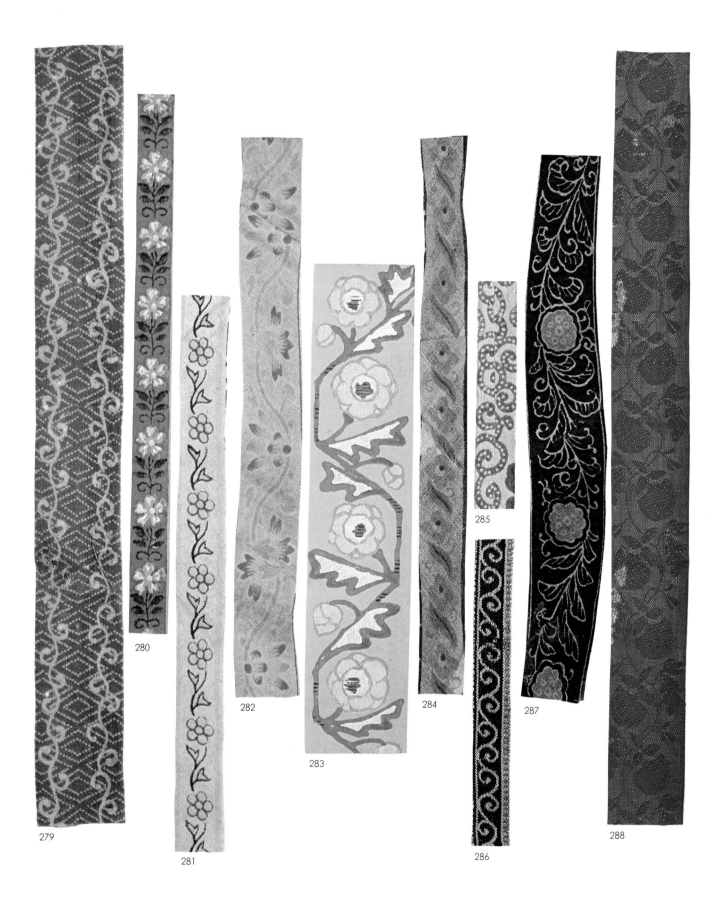

279

280

281

282

283

284

285

286

287

288

289

290

291

292

293

294

295

296

297

298

299

300

301

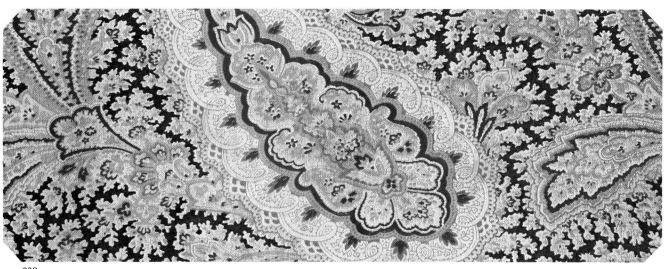

302

303

304

305

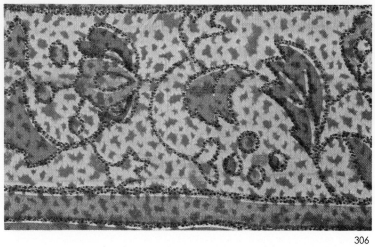

306

307

308

309

310

316

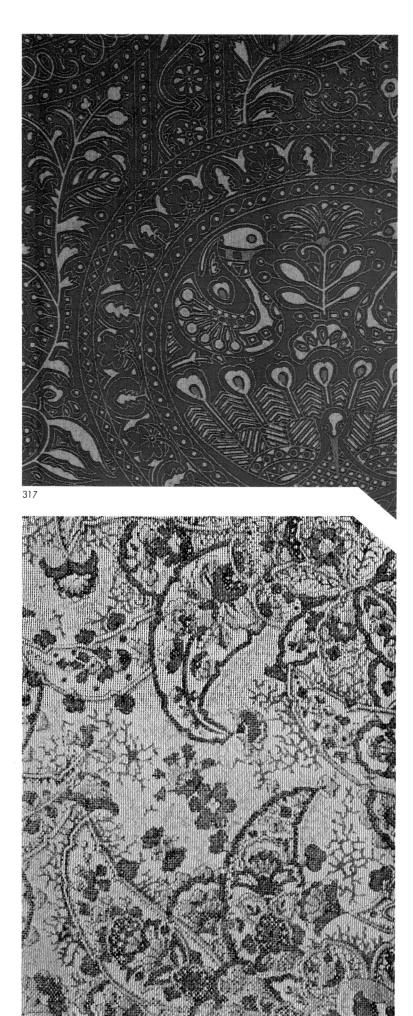

317

318

319

320

321

322

323

324

325

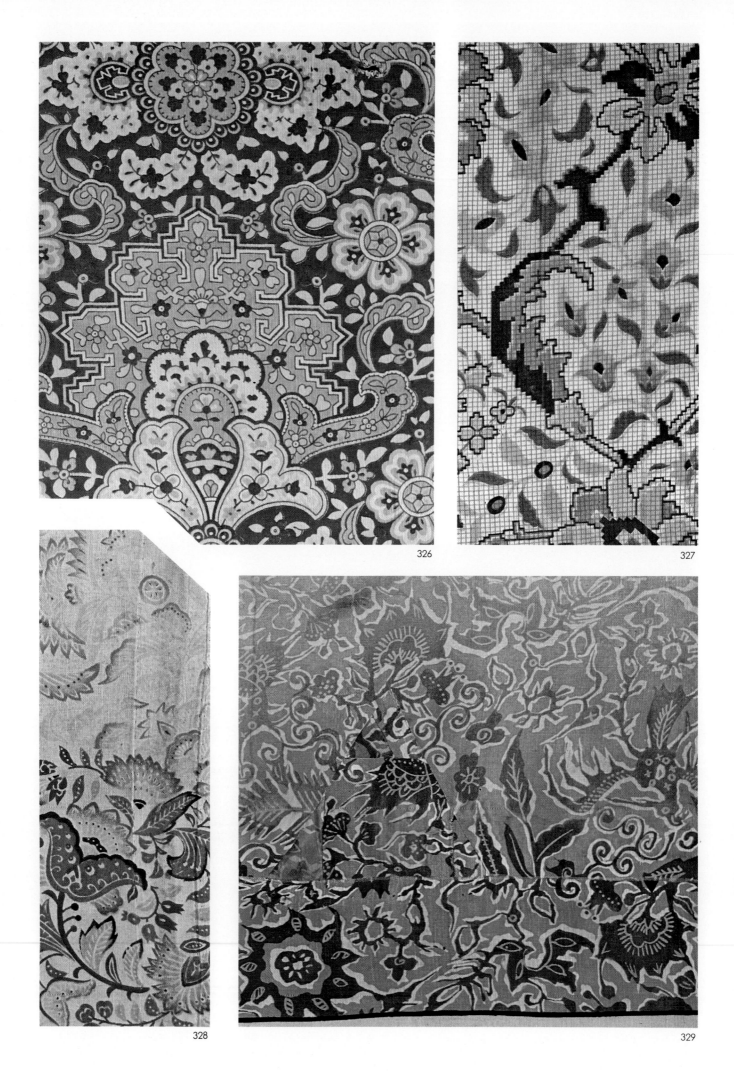

326

327

328

329

330

331

332

333

334

335

336

337

338

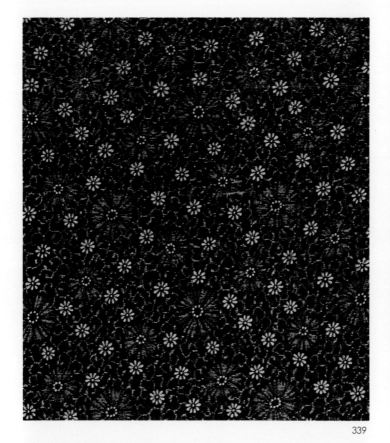

339

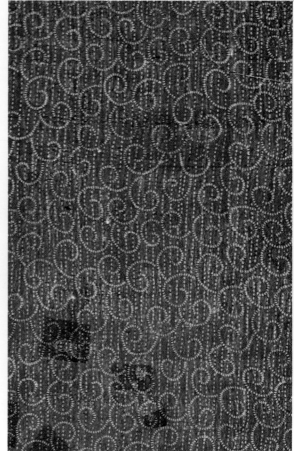

340

341

342

343

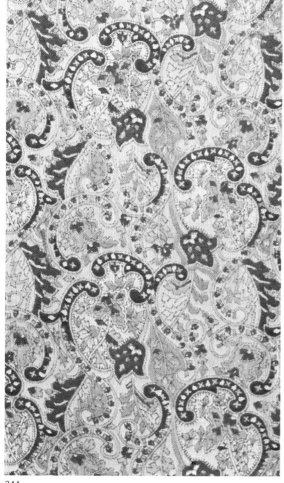

344

345

347

348

349

350

351

352

353

354

355

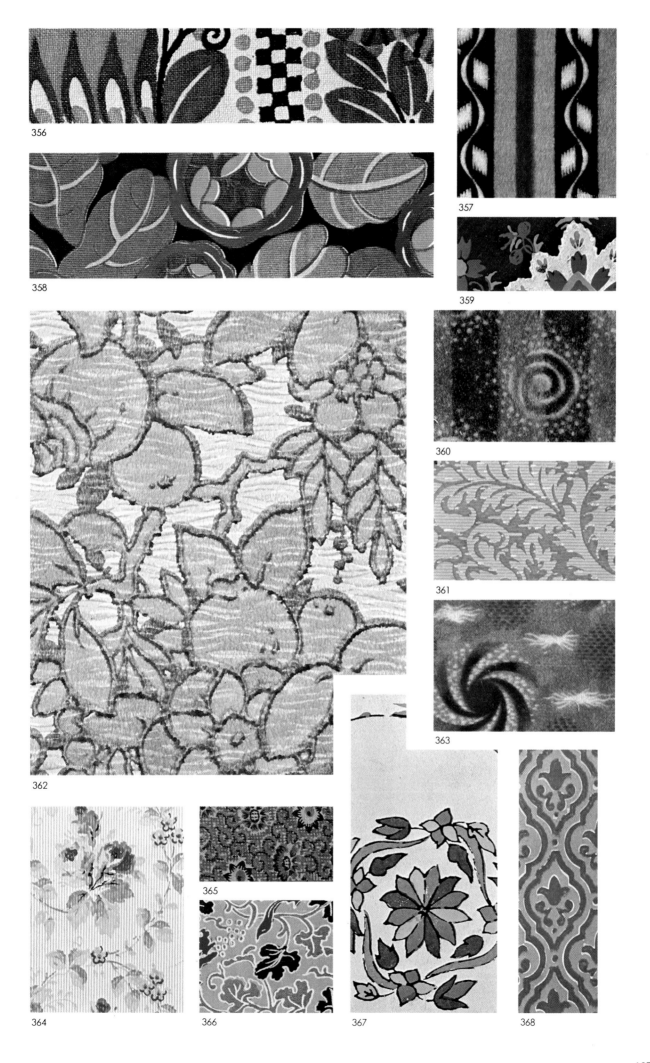

356

357

358

359

360

361

362

363

364

365

366

367

368

369

370

371

372

373

374

375

376

377

378

379

380

381

382

383

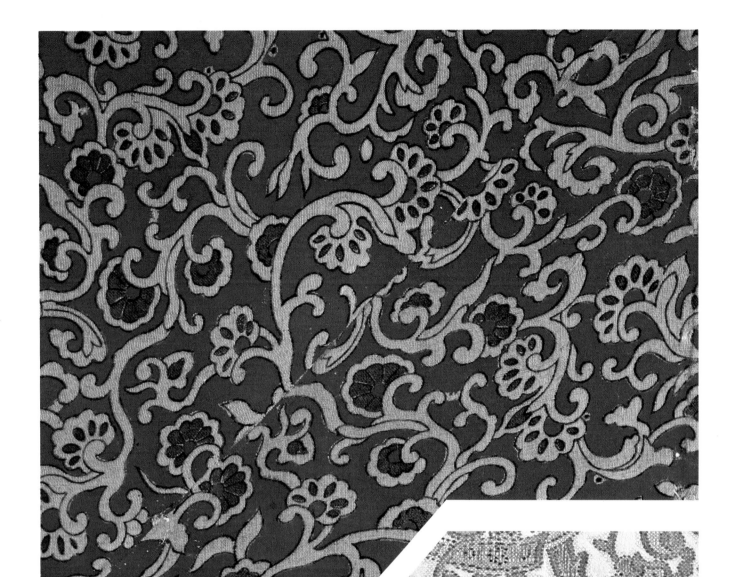

384

385

386

387

388

389

390

391

392

393

394

395

396

397

398

399

400

401

402

403

404

405

406

407

408

409

410

411

412

413

414

415

416

417

419

420

421

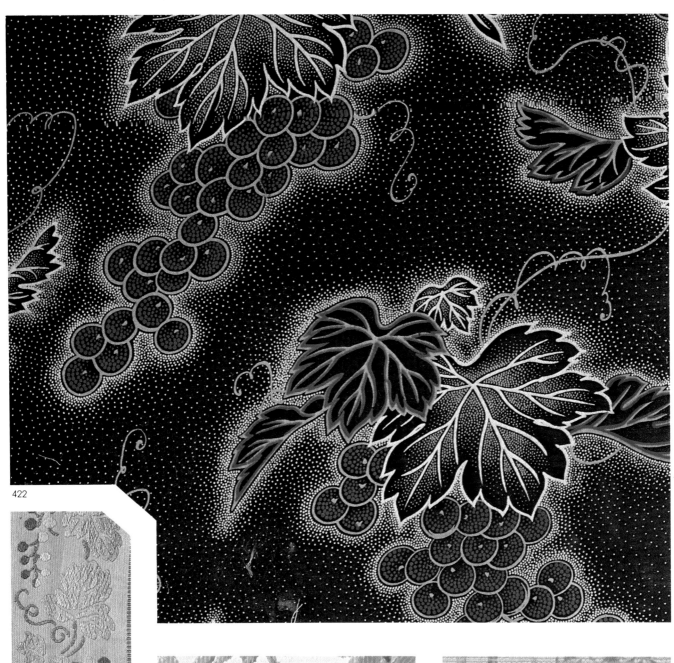

422

423

424

425

427

426

428

429

430

431

432

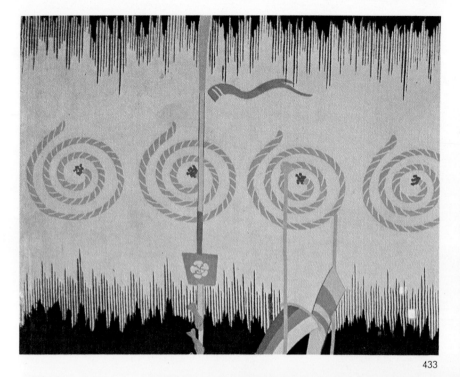

433

434

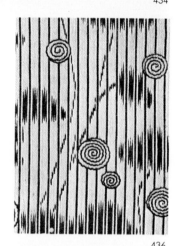

435

436

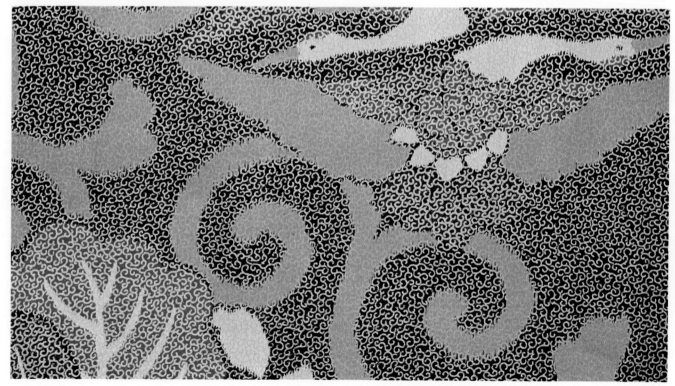

437

439

438

440

441

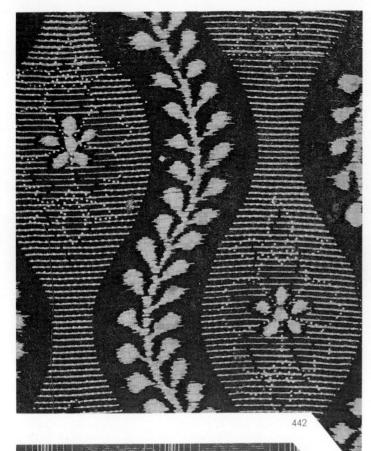

442

443

444

445

446

447

448

449

450

451

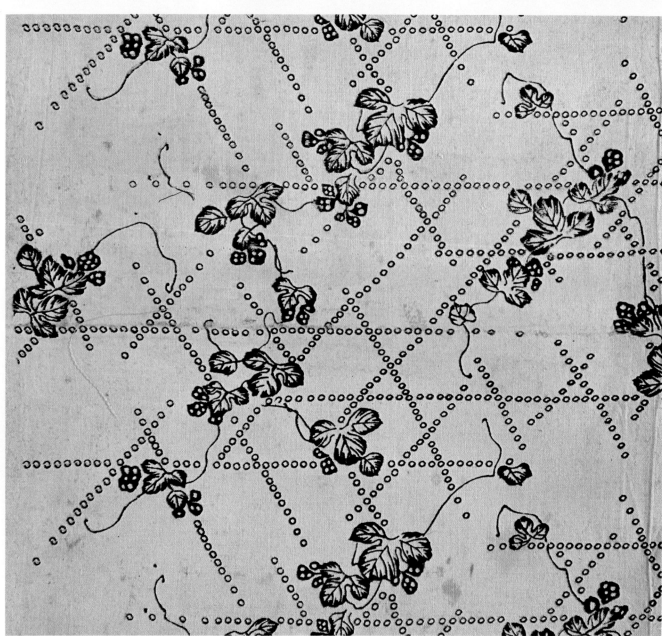

452

453

454

455

456

457

458

459

460

461

462

463

464

465

466

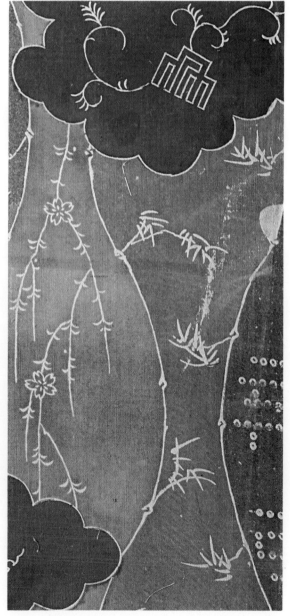

467

468

469

470

471

472

473

474

475

476

477

478

479

480

481

482

483

484

Vêtements ordinaires
(de type YUKATA, teint au patron)

485

486

487

488

489

490

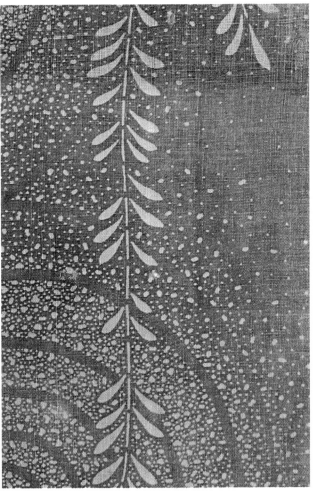

491

492

493

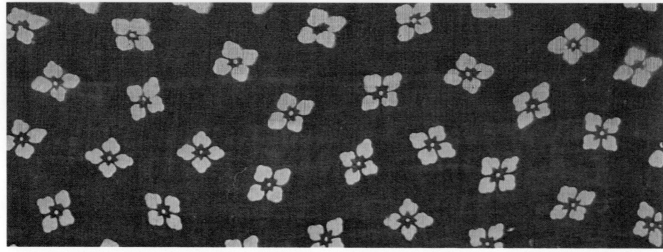

494

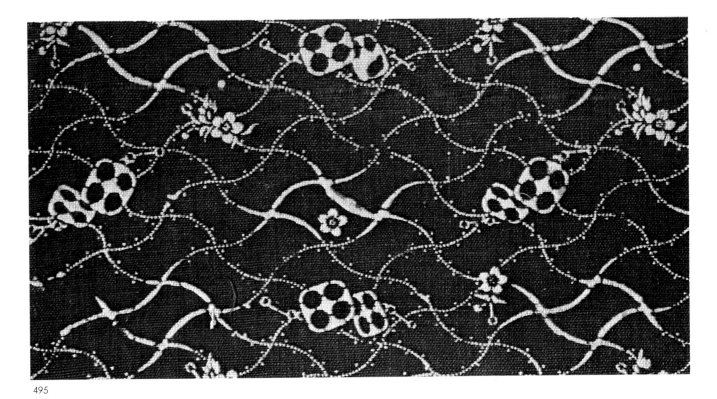

495

496

497

498

499

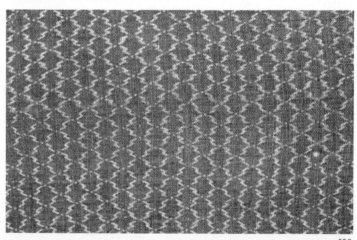

500

501

509

510

511

512

513

514

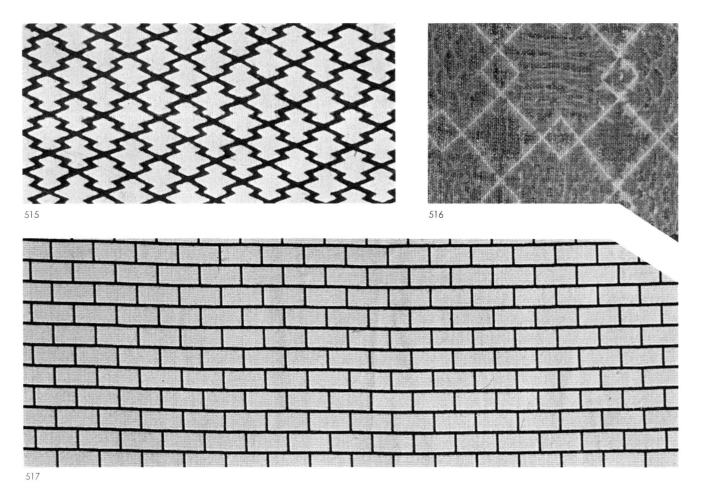

515

516

517

518

519

520

521

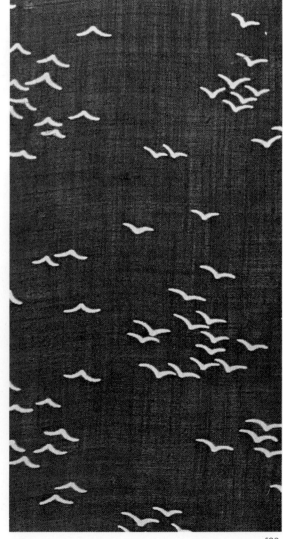

522

523

524

525

526

527

528

529

530

531

532

533

534

535

536

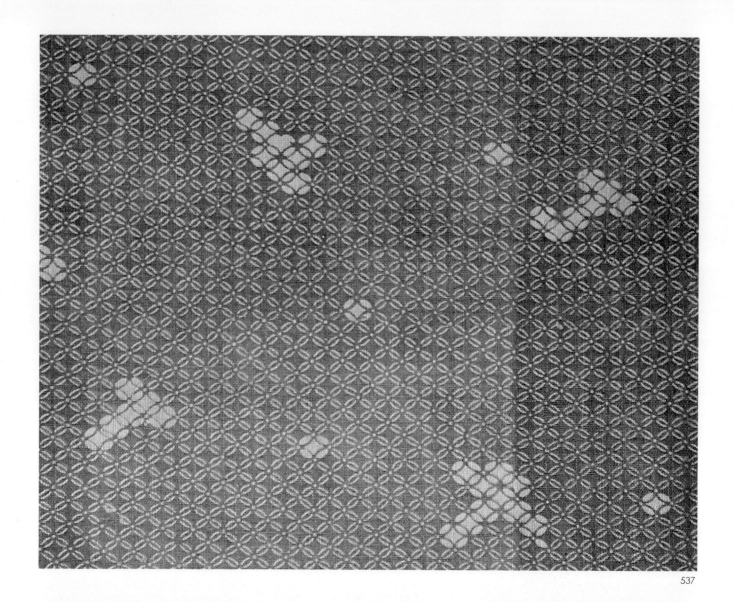

537

538

539

540

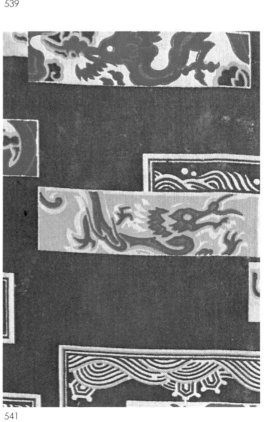

541

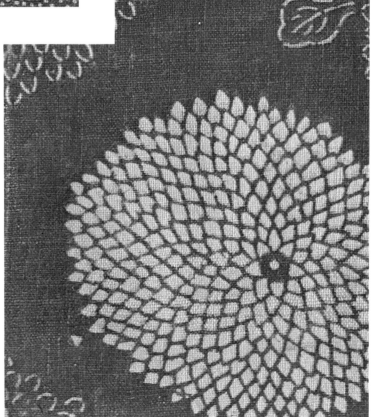

542

543

544

546

547

545

548

549

550

551

552

154